Little RIDDLERS

Essex

Edited By Connor Matthews

First published in Great Britain in 2018 by:

Young Writers
Remus House
Coltsfoot Drive
Peterborough
PE2 9BF
Telephone: 01733 890066
Website: www.youngwriters.co.uk

All Rights Reserved
Book Design by Ashley Janson
© Copyright Contributors 2018
SB ISBN 978-1-78896-372-5
Printed and bound in the UK by BookPrintingUK
Website: www.bookprintinguk.com
YB0358E

FOREWORD

Dear Reader,

Are you ready to get your thinking caps on to puzzle your way through this wonderful collection?

Young Writers' Little Riddlers competition set out to encourage young writers to create their own riddles. Their answers could be whatever or whoever their imaginations desired; from people to places, animals to objects, food to seasons. Riddles are a great way to further the children's use of poetic expression, including onomatopoeia and similes, as well as encourage them to 'think outside the box' by providing clues without giving the answer away immediately.

All of us here at Young Writers believe in the importance of inspiring young children to produce creative writing, including poetry, and we feel that seeing their own riddles in print will keep that creative spirit burning brightly and proudly.

We hope you enjoy riddling your way through this book as much as we enjoyed reading all the entries.

Connor Matthews
Editor

CONTENTS

Al-Noor Primary School, Ilford

Aishah Ghaffar Hakim (5)	1
M Ali Adeel (6)	2
Abdurrahman Bendjeddou (5)	3
Muhammad Ibrahim Ul Haque (5)	4
Ismah Siddiqa Alom (6)	5
Zayn Rahman (7)	6
Inayah Maryam Haque (6)	7
Mohammed Yasin Dhoomun (5)	8
Fatimah Az-Zahra Noor (6)	9
Danial Adam (7)	10
Sara Umer (6)	11
Madeeha Bint Noor (5)	12
Rayyan Hamidi (6)	13
Aasiya Khan (5)	14
Ilyas Chergui (6)	15
Sulaimaan Mohammad Asif (5)	16
Azizah Khan (5)	17
Hannaa Vaza (6)	18
Adyan Islam (6)	19
Abdullah El-Sayed (5)	20
Haneef Rahman (5)	21
Elias Zerouak (5)	22

Apex Primary School, Ilford

Sumayya Choudhury (7)	23
Koasar Mokhtari (8)	24
Sumayyah Ahsan (7)	25

Beehive Preparatory School, Redbridge

Amani Ahmed (5)	26
Tara Cambo (6)	27
Hayyaan Khan (5)	28
Harleen Kaur Kalyan (5)	29
Qamar Imtiaz (8)	30
Khalif Ali (5)	31
Sonakshi Tejasvini Singh (5)	32
Eesa Patel (6)	33
Arianna Digpal (5)	34
Zarak Imran (6)	35

Cherry Tree Primary & Nursery School, Basildon

Samuel (7)	36
Gavin Ferrera (6)	37
Alexa Sparkes (7)	38
Grace (6)	39
Nicholas Jasinski (6)	40
Callum Harry Stafford (6)	41
Ethan Szanto (6)	42
Aiden Michael Lee (6)	43
Makunga (7)	44
Jack Sutherland (7)	45
Brandon Wildman-Tutt (7)	46
Bailey Powlesland (7)	47
Libby Ann George (6)	48
Lois Walker (6)	49
Scott Mackenzie (7)	50
Sienna Polley (6)	51
Raya Tsvetanova (6)	52
Kimi Farenden (7)	53
George Cooper (6)	54

Amber Beckwith (7)	55
Joshua Gardner (7)	56
Kayce Battershall (6)	57
Joshua Crawford (7)	58
Mollie McCann (6)	59
Tegan Wallis (7)	60
Laycie (7)	61
Teddie Ronnie Collins (7)	62
Cody Lee Kiley (6)	63
Jesse Long (6)	64
Gracie-Leigh Grayston (7)	65
Matthew Dean (7)	66
Edward Jet Verrier (7)	67
Sofia (6)	68
Kye Sanders (7)	69
Ewan (7)	70
George Grey (6)	71
Nathan Bindeanu (6)	72
Amani lee (6)	73
Keitan Beechey (6)	74
Bobby (6)	75
Sebastian Cenciu (7)	76
Patric (7)	77

East Tilbury Infant School, Tilbury

Lilly Grace Davey (7)	78
Danielle McCann (6)	79
Abigail Yeldham (6)	80
Ava Wolfe (7)	81
Lexi Rose Ramsey (7)	82
Emily Rose Sibley (5)	83

Fingringhoe CE Primary School, Fingringhoe

Jack Seaman	84
Lily Anisha Patel (7)	85
Shaila LeBoutillier	86
Cynthia Elliott (7)	87
Lily Holmes (6)	88
Fern Fox (6)	89
Oscar Priestley (6)	90
Jack Cock	91

Dylan Roxby (6)	92
Tallulah Brice Fremel (6)	93
Riley Robinson-Amass	94
Olivia Rae (6)	95
Fin Mason (7)	96
Gracie Rose Carlsson (7)	97
Yasam Hope Violet Greenleaf (6)	98
Leo Hammarton (6)	99

Fordham All Saints CE Primary, Colchester

Yash Patel (4)	100
Sophie Carton (5)	101
Ezri Marsh (5)	102
Charlie Rowland (5)	103
Sophie Halls (4)	104
Aimee Rogers (5)	105
Riley Collar (5)	106
Freya Violet Moroney (4)	107
Oliver Bragger (4)	108
Lennon James Philip Rochester (5)	109
Henry Gurton (5)	110
Annabel Warland (4)	111
Jude Taylor (5)	112
Albert Lister (4)	113
Poppy Bragger (4)	114

Gearies Primary School, Gants Hill

Aribah Hossain Raida (6)	115
Anukriti Barot (6)	116
Aarshika Kokulan (6)	117
Sukhvir Singh Bassi (7)	118
Liyana Khan (6)	119
Krithi Rao Erabelli (7)	120
Milly Nakum (7)	121
Atharv Jadhav (7)	122
Inayah Iffat Hussain (7)	123
Rayyan Mukhtar (7)	124
Nadia Suleyman (7)	125
Josh Wigham (6)	126

Aarav Ravikiran (7)	127
Anshika Sinha (6)	128
Sukaina Shanawaz (7)	129
Aileen Ahmed (7)	130
Avneet Kaur Bansal (6)	131
Eshaal Shah (6)	132
Zakariya Mughal (7)	133
Aniya Rahman (7)	134
Faisal Shaikh (7)	135
Oluwaseyi Rebecca Olukoshi (6)	136
Reyansh Singh (6)	137
Rayyanah Rahman (6)	138
Nathan Joshua Sarusan Suthushan (7)	139
Moses Kwok (7)	140
Haniah Khan (7)	141
Jannat Ali (7)	142
Nikita Rayanagoudar (6)	143
Sneha Chawla (7)	144
Zakariya Ajaib (6)	145
Jake Sivadasan (6)	146
Rahim Khan (6)	147
Yan Mellies (6)	148
Eesa Koreshi (6)	149
Hamza Musa Islam (6)	150
Usaud Abdul-Hafiz (7)	151
Judi Ibrahim (6)	152
Huma Ali (7)	153
Ethan Arifin (7)	154

Holy Family Catholic Primary School, Benfleet

Vinnie Essex (6)	155
John Desireoluwa Akinlabi (6)	156
Elsie Mae Marsh (5)	157
Sam Chittock (5)	158
Milly McMeekin (6)	159
Jamie Scott (6)	160
Pearse Mastrogiacomo (6)	161
Alfie Robert Thomas (5)	162
Sam Starling (6)	163
Winnie Campbell (5)	164
Antonio Patron Fajardo (6)	165

Alicja Macleod (6)	166
Isabella Welling (6)	167
Leo Hanby (6)	168
Olivia Hope Ladyko (6)	169
Simon Patron Fajardo (6)	170
Tia Lily O'Callaghan (5)	171
Casper James Saban (5)	172
Ishika Jibi (6)	173
Roman Overall (5)	174
Tilly Witherall-Gosling (5)	175

Ingrave Johnstone CE Primary, Brentwood

Reece Oliver Newcombe (7)	176
Andrew Scott Gordon (7)	177
Lily Millington (6)	178
Matilda Rose Woodhouse (6)	179
Harley Emmie Brandon (6)	180
Adam Staunton (7)	181
Ronnie Tyler Smale (7)	182
Dylan Balroop (7)	183
Dylan Fox (7)	184
Nikita Jarkov (7)	185
Finley Pamment (6)	186
Frankie Towner (6)	187
Daniel Retief (7)	188
Elizabeth Ellery (7)	189
Frankie Harris (7)	190
Sehej Jutley (7)	191

THE POEMS

Little Riddlers 2018 - Essex

My Bright Shiny Wish

My mummy has one.
I so wish I had one too.
It's so white, big and shiny.
It looks so perfect with many sides.
It's so sparkly and bright just like the stars at night.
When the lights shineon it, the reflection is just so amazing.
White, pink, blue and red, it looks so beautiful.
I so wish I had one, but I am too young.
When I grow older I will wear one.
Maybe, if I'm lucky my daddy will buy me one!
What am I?

Answer: A diamond.

Aishah Ghaffar Hakim (5)
Al-Noor Primary School, Ilford

Bright And Bold

Sometimes I give comfort.
Sometimes I give pain.
I can show many colours.
Like a rainbow after rain.
I am powerful and strong.
I can destroy anything.
I love to eat, but hate to drink.
Death to me it will bring.
I am also useful.
I can make everything bright.
People use me for different things.
Don't ever question my might.
What am I?

Answer: Fire.

M Ali Adeel (6)
Al-Noor Primary School, Ilford

Can You Guess?

I belong to the big cats.
I do not miaow.
I am very fierce and I roar.
I am extremely dangerous.
I do not eat plants.
I do not climb high in the trees.
I do live within a pride.
My wife is called a lioness.
My babies are called cubs.
I am a mammal.
I am a meat eater.
I have a big mane.
I am the king of the jungle.
What am I?

Answer: A lion.

Abdurrahman Bendjeddou (5)
Al-Noor Primary School, Ilford

White And Bright

I come from the sky.
I am like a tiny white star.
I make everything white and bright.
You can find me everywhere.
When I come it gets cold everywhere.
Sometimes when it's sleet something cold falls down.
People play with me.
Children love me.
I make everyone happy.
I bring cold with me.
I shine, shine and shine.
What am I?

Answer: Snow.

Muhammad Ibrahim Ul Haque (5)
Al-Noor Primary School, Ilford

Read

I can make you cry
I can make you laugh.
You can take me anywhere,
even in the bath.
You will find people and places of every kind in me,
Just pick me up and see!
I usually stay in libraries and book bags.
Keep me for a little while or keep me forever.
Put me on your shelf and pick me up whenever.
What am I?

Answer: A book.

Ismah Siddiqa Alom (6)
Al-Noor Primary School, Ilford

What Am I?

I walk quieter than a mouse.
If you look tasty to me, I will eat you for dinner.
My eyes look like green emeralds.
I have fur like a winter coat.
Give me a tree to climb on,
I'm going to show how fast I go.
Try to find me but beware,
I'm darker than the darkest night.
What am I?

Answer: A black panther.

Zayn Rahman (7)
Al-Noor Primary School, Ilford

Hump

I am an animal.
They call me a mammal.
I can drink lots of water.
So I don't feel thirsty after a mile and a quarter.
People sometimes ride on me.
Sometimes I roam around free.
I have really long eyelashes to keep out the sand.
So I can see where I walk through desert land.
What am I?

Answer: A camel.

Inayah Maryam Haque (6)
Al-Noor Primary School, Ilford

The Speedy Runner

I am the largest bird in the world.
I'm a flightless bird.
I'm the only bird that has two toes on each foot.
I have long skinny legs.
I have a long neck with a dangerous beak.
I live in the wild in Africa.
I lay very big eggs.
I don't bury my head in the sand.
What am I?

Answer: An ostrich.

Mohammed Yasin Dhoomun (5)
Al-Noor Primary School, Ilford

Light Fluffy Clouds

I begin my life born in a meadow.
Sometimes I am white, sometimes I am yellow.
At times, I am sweet, and other times not.
I crackle and jump when I get hot.
I am sold in a box and shared amongst friends.
So, enjoy me with a film at the weekend!
What am I?

Answer: Popcorn.

Fatimah Az-Zahra Noor (6)
Al-Noor Primary School, Ilford

Super Cats

My fur is orange,
I am big and strong,
I roar so loud,
My favourite food is deer and lots more,
I hunt for my prey,
I live in Africa,
People like to hunt me,
I am stripy with black stripes.
What am I?

Answer: A tiger.

Danial Adam (7)
Al-Noor Primary School, Ilford

What Am I?

I have fur all over me.
The colour on my fur is black and orange stripes.
My fur is as soft as a fluffy pillow.
I can run very fast like a cheetah.
I have a long tail.
I can swim better than a shark.
What am I?

Answer: A tiger.

Sara Umer (6)
Al-Noor Primary School, Ilford

Season Of Winter

I like it when it's cold.
I like it when it snows.
The snowflakes are beautiful.
I have a juicy carrot for a nose.
I like to ice skate but I can't.
I miss the children when they go.
What am I?

Answer: A snowman.

Madeeha Bint Noor (5)
Al-Noor Primary School, Ilford

Red, Juicy And Sweet

I am red, juicy and sweet.
I am covered with seeds.
You can buy me in a shop
And eat me in a cupcake.
You can grow me in a garden.
When I am big and fresh
You can make me into jam.
What am I?

Answer: A strawberry.

Rayyan Hamidi (6)
Al-Noor Primary School, Ilford

The Queen Flower

I am a beautiful flower.
I grow taller in a rain shower.
I am like a rainbow.
I grow in different colours.
I am the queen flower.
I smell very nice.
Just be careful of my spikes.
What am I?

Answer: A rose.

Aasiya Khan (5)
Al-Noor Primary School, Ilford

Scary From The Past

I am scary, yet children like to play with me.
I existed on land years ago.
No one really knows how I lived and how I died.
When I am a movie star you can hear my roar!
What am I?

Answer: A dinosaur.

Ilyas Chergui (6)
Al-Noor Primary School, Ilford

Shiny White

I come in different shapes and sizes.
I come in many different colours.
I can be electric.
I can stick to the walls.
I can glow.
I am used for cleaning.
What am I?

Answer: A toothbrush.

Sulaimaan Mohammad Asif (5)
Al-Noor Primary School, Ilford

Legs In The Sea

I have a big head
I live in the ocean bed.
I have three hearts.
And I have eight long arms.
If you come close, I will blow you some ink.
Can you think what I am?

Answer: An octopus.

Azizah Khan (5)
Al-Noor Primary School, Ilford

What Am I?

I never forget and have a good brain.
I eat grass but don't like grain.
I have big ears.
But mice make me cry with tears.
I am quite big
What am I?

Answer: An elephant.

Hannaa Vaza (6)
Al-Noor Primary School, Ilford

Comfort Zone

I come in different sizes.
I can help you walk for miles.
I come in a pair.
I'm something that you wear.
With heels I am glam.
Can you guess what I am?

Answer: Shoes.

Adyan Islam (6)
Al-Noor Primary School, Ilford

Special Delivery

A mummy's love,
Sent from above,
Sweet as pie,
Coolness of her eyes.
A daddy's pride,
By his side,
All through life.
Who am I?

Answer: A baby.

Abdullah El-Sayed (5)
Al-Noor Primary School, Ilford

What Am I?

I have three lights
All in a row.
Red one means stop.
Yellow one means get ready.
Green one means go.
What am I?

Answer: A traffic light.

Haneef Rahman (5)
Al-Noor Primary School, Ilford

Roar!

I am scary.
I roar.
I have claws.
I love honey
I am furry.
I hunt for prey.
What am I?

Answer: A bear.

Elias Zerouak (5)
Al-Noor Primary School, Ilford

Swishy Swashy

I am beautiful and blue.
I am warm and salty too.
I am surrounded by countries.
And also continents.
I have seen historical world events.
My fish have fed Egyptian pharaohs,
And Roman armies.
Volcanoes have erupted near me.
But I have not had a tsunami.
What am I?

Answer: *The Mediterranean Sea.*

Sumayya Choudhury (7)
Apex Primary School, Ilford

Under The Ocean...

I am big and blue.
I have no legends this is true.
I want a fishy treat,
But will it be enough to eat?
I have a big family,
In the giant blue sea.
My tail will swish and swash,
How many sharks will I squash?
What am I?

Answer: The great blue whale.

Koasar Mokhtari (8)
Apex Primary School, Ilford

Up, Up And Away

I am covered in feathers.
I fly high in the sky in flocks.
I live in warm nests.
I have yellow feet, but no stinky socks.
I eat seeds and insects.
I can build a nest high up in the trees.
When I fly, I feel the cold breeze
What am I?

Answer: A bird.

Sumayyah Ahsan (7)
Apex Primary School, Ilford

Natural Beauty

I am a beautiful God's creation the world has ever seen.
I have colourful long feathers and I roost on a tree.
I feed on insects, berries and grains.
I can survive storms and monsoon rains.
I can live in your big garden, forest or park.
But I get frightened when a fox calls or a dog barks.
I can see life's wonders through my beautiful eyes.
What am I? With you it lies.

Answer: A peacock.

Amani Ahmed (5)
Beehive Preparatory School, Redbridge

Little Riddlers 2018 - Essex

Get Better

If you have a disaster,
I can give you a plaster.
If you are feeling blue, then I will check you.
If you have an infection,
I can give you an injection.
If you are ill, I can give you a pill.
When you are not feeling well,
I am someone who you can tell.
When you fall asleep.
I can check your heartbeat.
I won't make you feel worse,
Who am I?

Answer: A nurse.

Tara Cambo (6)
Beehive Preparatory School, Redbridge

The Bright Morning

I am white in colour.
I am soft in texture.
I appear in winter.
When it gets colder.
I melt in the sun.
But with me, children have fun.
I make children very cheerful.
When walking on me you have to be careful.
When you wake up in the morning
everything looks white.
What am I?

Answer: Snow.

Hayyaan Khan (5)
Beehive Preparatory School, Redbridge

The Weather

I am cold and beautiful.
In many countries I fall.
A snowman without me would be
nothing at all.
I am white and fluffy.
Before I become slushy.
I float down to the ground, without a sound.
When you wake up and see me.
You shout with delight.
What am I?

Answer: Snow.

Harleen Kaur Kalyan (5)
Beehive Preparatory School, Redbridge

Ride With Me

I come in all sizes, big or small.
I come in all colours, bright or cool.
I can take you anywhere you want to go.
Be that Westfield or your best friend's house.
I have a steering wheel inside
I have four wheels outside.
What am I?

Answer: A car.

Qamar Imtiaz (8)
Beehive Preparatory School, Redbridge

My Favourite Time

We go to the beach and it is very hot.
We have ice cream.
We have a nice fun day.
We can play outside and it's good.
We can have water fights.
Happy mums and dads and children
What is it?

Answer: The summer.

Khalif Ali (5)
Beehive Preparatory School, Redbridge

Pink

I stand tall and have a black and pink beak.
I am a good flyer.
I live all across the world.
When I go to bed,
I sleep on one leg.
I am named after my colour.
What am I?

Answer: A flamingo.

Sonakshi Tejasvini Singh (5)
Beehive Preparatory School, Redbridge

Sssss!

I am long.
I have no eyelids but I can still sleep.
I use my tongue to smell.
I squeeze my food tightly.
I am legless.
What am I?

Answer: A snake.

Eesa Patel (6)
Beehive Preparatory School, Redbridge

The Riddle

I am flat and sometimes bumpy
You can walk on forever
I am never-ending
I am round
You can travel everywhere on me
What am I?

Answer: *The world*

Arianna Digpal (5)
Beehive Preparatory School, Redbridge

Little Riddlers 2018 - Essex

Who Am I?

I start with a "P"
I end with an "E"
I have many letters.
What may I be?

Answer: A post office.

Zarak Imran (6)
Beehive Preparatory School, Redbridge

Clues About Animals

I have strong, sharp claws.
Most of the time I hunt my useless prey.
Surprisingly, I give everyone a big fright when I have a big roar!
My tail wiggles and waggles when I look hungry.
Fiercely my whiskers tingle when I hear animals.
My teeth are as sharp as the tip of a knife.
Mostly I hunt on my own.
I have black and orange stripes.
What am I?

Answer: A tiger.

Samuel (7)
Cherry Tree Primary & Nursery School, Basildon

The Mysterious Animal Swimming Underwater

I glide through the fresh, sky blue water as clear as glass.
I have a tail which flicks up and down.
I can travel hundreds of miles.
I've got eyes which gleam brightly like the sun.
I spray fresh water in the air like a fountain.
I have kind teeth as shiny as paper in the sun.
I have the shape of an oval and bare skin.
What am I?

Answer: A blue whale.

Gavin Ferrera (6)
Cherry Tree Primary & Nursery School, Basildon

What Am I?

I have a long neck that will help me drink and eat.
All the time I eat very slowly and so does my family.
My back and my body is really spotty and my family is too.
My tongue is very helpful, because I can wrap it around leaves.
I can be found in a zoo.
I am very tall, so I can see far away.
What am I?

Answer: A giraffe.

Alexa Sparkes (7)
Cherry Tree Primary & Nursery School, Basildon

A Riddle

I like to play with different people.
I like to lick them when we stop playing.
I like to run around chasing my fluffy bushy tail!
I am a pet and can be a rescue pet.
I am happy when I see people.
I chew on toys and teddies when my teeth hurt.
I like to eat bones.
I can say woof woof.
What am I?

Answer: A dog.

Grace (6)
Cherry Tree Primary & Nursery School, Basildon

The Colourful Flyer

I have fluffy wings as a copper and peach teddy bear.
I have gloomy fuschia, cherry legs like a colourful bird in the tree.
I have a milky, peach tail which swishes in the wind.
I have a ruby-rose glittery horn that makes wishes come true.
I have copper, ochre fur that waves in the wind slowly.
What am I?

Answer: A unicorn.

Nicholas Jasinski (6)
Cherry Tree Primary & Nursery School, Basildon

What Am I?

I am as grey as a stormy cloud.
You might find me in a jungle.
Some animals are friendly and nasty.
I eat fruit and trees as tall as a house.
Sometimes you can find me in hot places like Africa.
I have four legs that can crush hard things.
I have no arms.
I have a long trunk.
What am I?

Answer: An elephant.

Callum Harry Stafford (6)
Cherry Tree Primary & Nursery School, Basildon

The Fast Rider

I have wheels that are as shiny as gold.
I have a warm, cosy seat as smooth
as a teddy.
I have lots of people ride on me for miles.
I have a chain that connects
the two wheels.
I have a bell, so people in cars know
I'm there.
I have pedals so I can move fast or slow.
What am I?

Answer: A bike.

Ethan Szanto (6)
Cherry Tree Primary & Nursery School, Basildon

The Fabulous Hunter

I have a tail as long as a snake.
I have teeth as sharp as shiny, pointy pins.
I have four feet that make me speedy and fast.
I have a roar as loud as a thunderous storm.
I have sensitive ears that can hear everything near.
I have colourful stripes that make me look colourful.
What am I?

Answer: A tiger.

Aiden Michael Lee (6)
Cherry Tree Primary & Nursery School, Basildon

What Am I?

I have a trumpet and I catch dreams.
My best friend is Sophie and she is a little girl.
I go to catch dreams alone and I am a real person.
I drink Frobscottle.
I am a giant and I live in a giant country.
Other giants are mean to me.
I am a kind giant but the others are not.
Who am I?

Answer: *The BFG.*

Makunga (7)
Cherry Tree Primary & Nursery School, Basildon

The Good Treat

I make a good treat with icing on.
I have a strawberry that is crimson and maroon.
I have thick layers to make it easier to cut.
I am good for tasting with delicious slices.
I am yummy for a treat.
I am a good treat for birthdays.
I am amazing and scrumptious
What am I?

Answer: A strawberry cake.

Jack Sutherland (7)
Cherry Tree Primary & Nursery School, Basildon

What Am I?

I have sharp teeth and I'm small.
Usually I am out hunting.
I'm not friendly.
I like hot weather.
I sometimes have cubs.
I don't like water.
People are scared of me when I growl at them.
Surprisingly, I'm the fastest land animal in the world.
What am I?

Answer: A cheetah.

Brandon Wildman-Tutt (7)
Cherry Tree Primary & Nursery School, Basildon

What Am I?

You can find me in the jungle.
I have soft, smooth fur but you cannot pet me,
I might go crazy.
I'm funny and surprisingly, I am found in some leaves in the hazel trees.
I eat bananas because they taste delicious.
I swing from tree to tree.
I am cheeky.
What am I?

Answer: A monkey.

Bailey Powlesland (7)
Cherry Tree Primary & Nursery School, Basildon

What Am I?

My teeth are sharp and snappy.
I am green and spiky.
When it is night time, I sneak up on delicious fish and eat them.
Sometimes you can find me in the lake.
Most animals have fur, I have bumpy skin.
People say I am mean as can be.
I am very dangerous.
What am I?

Answer: A crocodile.

Libby Ann George (6)
Cherry Tree Primary & Nursery School, Basildon

The Fast Mover

I have small grey doll wheels as small as an ant.
I have tiny, raven handles as tiny as a buzzing bee.
I am as fast as a shiny silver car.
I am as solid as a piece of metal.
I am the best at tricks.
I have tiny rock-solid handles as hard as metal.
What am I?

Answer: A scooter.

Lois Walker (6)
Cherry Tree Primary & Nursery School, Basildon

What Am I?

I am a herbivore that likes to climb trees.
I am very small but very clever.
In our country I am really grey.
But in other countries I have other colours.
I am an animal that always eats nuts and acorns.
My tail is bushy and usually found in forests.
What am I?

Answer: A squirrel.

Scott Mackenzie (7)
Cherry Tree Primary & Nursery School, Basildon

What Am I?

My habitat is the wild African savannah.
Usually my autumn colours camouflage me in the long grass.
I sometimes sleep in the trees.
When I am hungry I silently creep up on my prey.
I am one of the big five.
I am the fastest land animal in the world.
What am I?

Answer: A cheetah.

Sienna Polley (6)
Cherry Tree Primary & Nursery School, Basildon

The Scratcher

I have sharp, milky, golden claws as sharp as a knife.
I have snowy, ivory fur as soft as a cloud.
I have a wiggly, copper, coral tail.
I have pointy black whiskers.
I have lime green eyes.
I have a family.
I have pointy peach and copper ears.
What am I?

Answer: A cat.

Raya Tsvetanova (6)
Cherry Tree Primary & Nursery School, Basildon

What Am I?

I am a type of bird that is brown and fluffy.
People can find me in my nest covering my rigid blue eggs.
I am a bird that can't fly.
I live in New Zealand.
Surprisingly I only move in winter to stay warm.
I can't be kept as a pet.
What am I?

Answer: A kiwi bird.

Kimi Farenden (7)
Cherry Tree Primary & Nursery School, Basildon

What Am I?

Every day I eat emerald, delicious grass,
berries and leaves.
I wander about all the time.
I've got an ivory spiky horn to scare people.
My ears are extremely floppy.
Every single time my tail goes swish.
All the time my body is massive.
What am I?

Answer: A rhino.

George Cooper (6)
Cherry Tree Primary & Nursery School, Basildon

What Am I?

I work in the jungle alone.
I am scary.
Usually my eyes glow in the dark.
My eyes are as green as grass.
My paws are white and very sharp.
My teeth are chalky and sharp.
So beware.
I live in the jungle.
I have ebony stripes.
What am I?

Answer: A tiger.

Amber Beckwith (7)
Cherry Tree Primary & Nursery School, Basildon

Fast Runner

I have a rocky, wiggly tail.
I have fast legs that are yellow.
My teeth are sharp as a knife.
I catch my prey by hiding in the swaying green grass.
I am very scary.
Everyone is scared of my claws.
I have stripes on my back and belly.
What am I?

Answer: A tiger.

Joshua Gardner (7)
Cherry Tree Primary & Nursery School, Basildon

What Am I?

I am very greedy and I eat leaves.
I am often found in a zoo or in Africa.
My tongue is often purple and very long.
I am not a pet so people can't keep me.
My nose is very big.
I'm very friendly to people.
I am very tall.
What am I?

Answer: A giraffe.

Kayce Battershall (6)
Cherry Tree Primary & Nursery School, Basildon

The Red Plant

I have jet-black holes on me.
I am as red as I can be.
I have green leaves on me.
I grow on an emerald green bush.
I am as juicy as an apple
I can be in a scrumptious salad.
I have the jet-black ravens trying to eat me.
Who can I be?

Answer: A strawberry.

Joshua Crawford (7)
Cherry Tree Primary & Nursery School, Basildon

The Milk Drinker

I have pointy sharp claws as sharp as a knife.
I have smooth peach fur, it keeps me warm at night.
I have a wet nose.
I have two ears as pointy as a knife.
I have long thin whiskers, so bendy.
I have big wide eyes as big as an owl.
What am I?

Answer: A cat.

Mollie McCann (6)
Cherry Tree Primary & Nursery School, Basildon

Soft Sweet Treat

I am sometimes sweet or sour.
I am called a cup, but you can't drink out of me.
I am soft as a cloud.
I can be crunchy when you overheat me.
I have colourful toppings and I can be sparkly.
I sometimes have candles.
What am I?

Answer: A cupcake.

Tegan Wallis (7)
Cherry Tree Primary & Nursery School, Basildon

What Am I?

I am brown and like nuts.
I sometimes live in trees because I like branches.
I don't eat meat it is horrible.
I don't like strawberries, only nuts.
When I see people, I get shy.
I have a tail with fur on it.
What am I?

Answer: A squirrel.

Laycie (7)
Cherry Tree Primary & Nursery School, Basildon

The Little Green Animal

I am as green as trees.
I like to swim in water.
I have sticky hands and feet.
I have a long pink tongue.
I like to splash in water.
I am as small as a turtle.
I like to jump as high as I can.
What am I?

Answer: A frog.

Teddie Ronnie Collins (7)
Cherry Tree Primary & Nursery School, Basildon

A Flying Red Beast

He has rose-red big wings.
He has eyebrows as black as smoke.
He has sharp feet as sharp as knives.
He has a mouth as big as a finger.
He has feet as big as a giant block.
He has a humongous tail
What am I?

Answer: A dragon.

Cody Lee Kiley (6)
Cherry Tree Primary & Nursery School, Basildon

Shiny Stuff

I have something that every building has.
I am as bright as a puddle and bright metal.
I have a person looking at me every single day.
I have glass.
I am always shiny.
I can have a curtain.
What am I?

Answer: A window.

Jesse Long (6)
Cherry Tree Primary & Nursery School, Basildon

The Great Singing

I have a black jacket.
My singing is as soft as a bird.
My shoes are green.
My hair is ginger like an orange.
My guitar is smooth.
I wear silky smooth glasses that shine
in the sun.
Who am I?

Answer: Ed Sheeran.

Gracie-Leigh Grayston (7)
Cherry Tree Primary & Nursery School, Basildon

What Am I?

I am hot.
I am as bright as a big pot of paint.
I am yellow like a banana.
I am big and round like an elephant.
I have shining, amber beams that people see.
I am in the beautiful blue sky.
What am I?

Answer: The sun.

Matthew Dean (7)
Cherry Tree Primary & Nursery School, Basildon

The Quick Mover

I have giant, black wheels.
I have unusual handles.
I have solid walls as shiny as a knight.
I have bright lights.
I have windows as clear as a door.
I am as fast as a cheetah in the wild.
What am I?

Answer: A car.

Edward Jet Verrier (7)
Cherry Tree Primary & Nursery School, Basildon

What Am I?

I have a fluffy soft body.
I love to drink icy milk.
I have whiskers.
I love to sniff.
I like to chase mice and birds.
I have sharp claws.
I have sharp teeth.
I say miaow.
What am I?

Answer: A cat.

Sofia (6)
Cherry Tree Primary & Nursery School, Basildon

What Am I?

I am a poisonous animal.
I am thin and long.
I have no hands or legs.
I am often found near water in the jungle.
I have a long tongue and I hiss.
I have stripes and a long body.
What am I?

Answer: A snake.

Kye Sanders (7)
Cherry Tree Primary & Nursery School, Basildon

What Am I?

I live in a mysterious jungle.
I like to climb gigantic trees.
Mostly I am friendly.
I run very fast.
Sometimes, my cheeks can get bigger and bigger.
I like to eat nuts.
What am I?

Answer: A squirrel

Ewan (7)
Cherry Tree Primary & Nursery School, Basildon

What Am I?

I am really spotty.
Sometimes I live in Africa.
My babies are called cubs.
I am rapid and I am the fastest animal.
I hunt for my prey.
Usually I sleep in a pack.
What am I?

Answer: A cheetah.

George Grey (6)
Cherry Tree Primary & Nursery School, Basildon

What Am I?

I like to eat small animals.
Sometimes I curl up.
I have no arms or legs.
I am long.
I am slippery
I have no feet.
I live in long grass near a tree.
What am I?

Answer: A snake.

Nathan Bindeanu (6)
Cherry Tree Primary & Nursery School, Basildon

What Am I?

I am small and I am cute.
I have four fluffy paws.
I like to play.
I live in a house.
I like to eat kibble.
I like to go to the park.
I like to bark
What am I?

Answer: A pug.

Amani lee (6)
Cherry Tree Primary & Nursery School, Basildon

What Am I?

I live in hot countries.
I am big.
I have big ears.
I am grey.
I eat plants.
You can see me at the zoo.
I have a trunk.
What am I?

Answer: An elephant.

Keitan Beechey (6)
Cherry Tree Primary & Nursery School, Basildon

What Am I?

I eat meat.
I'm the king of the jungle.
I have the loudest roar ever.
I have claws.
I'm yellow.
I have furry hair.
What am I?

Answer: A lion.

Bobby (6)
Cherry Tree Primary & Nursery School, Basildon

What Am I?

I am so strong.
I live in Africa
I have four paws.
I like to eat game meat.
I like to hunt.
When I call I roar.
What am I?

Answer: A lion.

Sebastian Cenciu (7)
Cherry Tree Primary & Nursery School, Basildon

What Am I?

I am strong.
I have a tail.
I live in Africa.
I like to eat meat.
My young are called cubs.
I roar!
What am I?

Answer: A lion.

Patric (7)
Cherry Tree Primary & Nursery School, Basildon

Changes

I am around all year round.
I make pretty flowers appear and the birds sing happily.
Paddling pools, water fights and ice creams
All enjoyed when I'm around.
I turn leaves from green to shades of orange, red and brown.
As you watch them fall from the trees.
I change again this time I bring
frost and snow.
What am I?

Answer: *The seasons.*

Lilly Grace Davey (7)
East Tilbury Infant School, Tilbury

Goodbye

I'm cuddly and also cold.
I'm always young and never old.
My nose is something you can eat.
If you look, I have no feet.
Play for an hour or play for a day.
But when the sun comes out I go away.
My brown arms wave goodbye.
I do miss you.
What am I?

Answer: A snowman.

Danielle McCann (6)
East Tilbury Infant School, Tilbury

Abi's Favourite Trick

I teach children.
I play games in the garden and in the classroom.
I teach many lessons.
I like to make lessons fun.
I can be quite strict.
I am quite amazing and fun.
I teach the after school club computing.
Who am I?

Answer: Mr Powell.

Abigail Yeldham (6)
East Tilbury Infant School, Tilbury

Naughty Or Nice?

You hardly ever see me.
But you know I have a beard.
Even though I come late at night.
I am not feared.
I don't get into houses by walking through the front door.
Instead I come down chimneys.
Who am I?

Answer: Father Christmas.

Ava Wolfe (7)
East Tilbury Infant School, Tilbury

Magic Beasts

She is magic and kind and beautiful too.
You would be lucky to see her colours like a rainbow,
Her hair is so long.
She is elegant and graceful.
She shows herself only in magic.
She is fictional.
What is she?

Answer: A unicorn.

Lexi Rose Ramsey (7)
East Tilbury Infant School, Tilbury

Animal Wonders

I climb trees, but I am not a cat.
I hibernate, but I am not a bear.
I eat nuts, but I am not a bird.
I'm a type of rodent, but I'm not a rat.
I have a bushy tail, but I'm not a fox.
What am I?

Answer: A squirrel.

Emily Rose Sibley (5)
East Tilbury Infant School, Tilbury

Hunting, Hungry

I like to eat insects and grains.
You can find me in the open woodlands.
I have a soft under side.
I shuffle along.
If you touch me you might get hurt.
I am miniature.
I burrow down in the ground to sleep.
What am I?

Answer: A hedgehog.

Jack Seaman
Fingringhoe CE Primary School, Fingringhoe

Holly

I have about five thousand spikes.
Fleas live in my spikes.
I normally live in burrows.
I like seeds and insects.
I like playing in grasslands.
I am nocturnal.
People think I am cute.
What am I?

Answer: A hedgehog.

Lily Anisha Patel (7)
Fingringhoe CE Primary School, Fingringhoe

The Hungry, Hunted

I eat baby birds and snails.
I have five thousand spikes.
I am shy.
I am nocturnal because I don't like the sun.
I like digging holes.
If you touch me, you might get hurt.
What am I?

Answer: A hedgehog.

Shaila LeBoutillier

Fingringhoe CE Primary School, Fingringhoe

The Riddle

I have five thousand spikes.
I live in burrows in open woodlands.
I eat insects, seeds and grains.
I am nocturnal.
I like playing in meadows.
I scurry along the floor.
What am I?

Answer: A hedgehog.

Cynthia Elliott (7)
Fingringhoe CE Primary School, Fingringhoe

Spiky, Hungry

I live in forests.
I have a small, black nose.
I like to eat slugs, snails and worms.
I am an omnivore.
I eat insects and I am nocturnal.
I lose my spikes once a year.
What am I?

Answer: A hedgehog.

Lily Holmes (6)
Fingringhoe CE Primary School, Fingringhoe

Snappy Animal

I have sharp, bloody teeth.
I am bumpy with a long, snappy mouth.
I have a cold body
and you don't want to see me.
I go under the water.
I have a squishy tail.
What am I?

Answer: A crocodile.

Fern Fox (6)
Fingringhoe CE Primary School, Fingringhoe

Snappy, Spiky

I am gigantic.
I have spikes on my back.
I have sharp teeth and lots of them.
I can pretend I am a floating log.
I have a muscular tail.
I have a long mouth.
What am I?

Answer: A crocodile.

Oscar Priestley (6)
Fingringhoe CE Primary School, Fingringhoe

Crunchy

I eat fish.
I snap.
I have sharp teeth.
I have spikes on my back.
I have a long wavy tail.
I have powerful jaws.
I snap like lightning.
What am I?

Answer: A crocodile.

Jack Cock
Fingringhoe CE Primary School, Fingringhoe

Henry

I have five thousand spines.
I sleep through winter.
I live underground.
I move slowly.
I go out at night.
I have a soft underbelly.
What am I?

Answer: A hedgehog.

Dylan Roxby (6)
Fingringhoe CE Primary School, Fingringhoe

Spooky

I am shy.
People think I like cheese but I don't.
My nose is miniscule.
I eat fifteen to twenty times a day.
I scurry along everywhere.
What am I?

Answer: A mouse.

Tallulah Brice Fremel (6)
Fingringhoe CE Primary School, Fingringhoe

Cute, Cheeky Geoffry

I like hiding in the hay bales.
People think I like cheese, but I don't.
I scurry along.
I like eating scraps.
I'm tiny.
What am I?

Answer: A mouse.

Riley Robinson-Amass
Fingringhoe CE Primary School, Fingringhoe

Hunting

I eat meat and I hunt.
I have a fluffy mane.
I have yellowy golden fur.
I drink blood.
I live in Africa.
I hunt for meat.
What am I?

Answer: A lion.

Olivia Rae (6)
Fingringhoe CE Primary School, Fingringhoe

Dave

I am very shy.
I have round eyes.
I live in the water
I'm very colourful.
I don't like the day.
What am I?

Answer: A crocodile.

Fin Mason (7)
Fingringhoe CE Primary School, Fingringhoe

Nosy

I am very shy.
I come out at night.
People think I like cheese.
Lions are scared of me.
I have round ears.
What am I?

Answer: A mouse.

Gracie Rose Carlsson (7)
Fingringhoe CE Primary School, Fingringhoe

Rosy

I have sharp teeth.
I have a fluffy mane.
I am fierce.
I have flesh-tearing jaws.
I am huge.
What am I?

Answer: A lion.

Yasam Hope Violet Greenleaf (6)
Fingringhoe CE Primary School, Fingringhoe

Scurrying

I'm very shy.
I like to live in sheds.
I eat scraps.
I have a long tail.
What am I?

Answer: A mouse.

Leo Hammarton (6)
Fingringhoe CE Primary School, Fingringhoe

Roar!

I am (was) as tall as the school hall.
I have a long, strong tail
My teeth are as sharp as scissors.
I make an awesome sound.
Nnng... Arr... Err!
I have hard skin to protect me with small spikes on my spine and tail.
My eyes are green like leaves on a tree.
I'm not around now, but I lived millions of years ago!
What am I?

Answer: A T-rex

Yash Patel (4)
Fordham All Saints CE Primary, Colchester

The Hunter!

I could live in a farm or in a house.
I have a long, fluffy tail.
I have long whiskers.
I have special eyes that can see at night.
I sharpen my claws on wood.
I have four feet.
I like to pounce on mice!
What am I?

Answer: A cat.

Sophie Carton (5)
Fordham All Saints CE Primary, Colchester

Happy Feet!

I live at the very bottom of the world,
I like to catch fish in the freezing water.
I have two flippers.
I have a beak.
I huddle together with my friends.
What am I?

Answer: A penguin.

Ezri Marsh (5)
Fordham All Saints CE Primary, Colchester

… Little Riddlers 2018 - Essex

Clippity Clop

I like to eat grass, carrots and apples.
I can stand up when I am asleep.
I like to run, pull carts and be ridden.
I have four legs, a swishy tail and a mane.
What am I?

Answer: A horse.

Charlie Rowland (5)
Fordham All Saints CE Primary, Colchester

Let It Go!

I have white hair that is in a plait.
My dress is blue and it sparkles.
I am freezing cold and turn things to ice.
I can make a palace out of ice.
Who am I?

Answer: Elsa from Frozen.

Sophie Halls (4)
Fordham All Saints CE Primary, Colchester

Down On The Farm

I am fluffy.
I am as white as snow.
I live on a farm.
I like to play with my brothers and sisters.
I have four woolly legs.
I go baa! Baa!
What am I?

Answer: A lamb.

Aimee Rogers (5)
Fordham All Saints CE Primary, Colchester

Driving In My Car!

I am as red as a fire engine.
I have four tyres.
I like to race fast.
My best friend is a tow truck.
Riley thinks I am the best!
Who am I?

Answer: Lightning McQueen.

Riley Collar (5)
Fordham All Saints CE Primary, Colchester

Night, Night!

I wear a pink dress.
I love to sleep.
I have a crown.
I don't like needles because they hurt my finger!
I married a prince.
Who am I?

Answer: Sleeping Beauty.

Freya Violet Moroney (4)
Fordham All Saints CE Primary, Colchester

Emergency!

I drive a red truck.
I have to wear a helmet.
Saving people is my favourite.
I sometimes need a ladder.
Sometimes I get really hot.
Who am I?

Answer: A fireman.

Oliver Bragger (4)
Fordham All Saints CE Primary, Colchester

Miaow! Miaow!

I like to roar!
I am orange and black.
I am stripy like a zebra crossing.
I have four feet with claws.
I live in the wild.
What am I?

Answer: A tiger.

Lennon James Philip Rochester (5)
Fordham All Saints CE Primary, Colchester

Freezing!

I can swim and slide.
I am black and white.
I cannot fly but I am a bird.
I have flippers.
I live in a very cold place!
What am I?

Answer: A penguin.

Henry Gurton (5)
Fordham All Saints CE Primary, Colchester

In The Arctic

I hunt for food.
I live in the coldness.
I have pointy ears like sticks
I am white.
I like to stay with my babies!
Who am I?

Answer: An Arctic fox.

Annabel Warland (4)
Fordham All Saints CE Primary, Colchester

Precious

I eat trees and leaves.
I am black and white.
I look like I wear a mask.
You would find me in Africa.
I have a tail.
What am I?

Answer: A zebra.

Jude Taylor (5)
Fordham All Saints CE Primary, Colchester

Wiggly Woo!

I like to wiggle.
I live in mud.
I am pink like a flower.
I am a tasty dinner for birds.
I am slimy.
What am I?

Answer: A worm.

Albert Lister (4)
Fordham All Saints CE Primary, Colchester

Stripy

I have stripes.
My eyes are big.
I have baby cubs.
I am orange.
I have long whiskers.
What am I?

Answer: A tiger.

Poppy Bragger (4)
Fordham All Saints CE Primary, Colchester

The Scary Thing

My teeth are as sharp as sharks' teeth.
My roar is like a dragon but even louder.
I eat lots of meat.
I live in a cave in the jungle.
My colours are yellow and brown.
I live in a hot country like Africa.
I have four legs and four paws.
My legs can run very fast.
My ears are as soft as snow.
What am I?

Answer: A lion.

Aribah Hossain Raida (6)
Gearies Primary School, Gants Hill

The Invisible Thing

I live inside you.
I know everything you say.
You can talk with me.
I do what you do.
I look beautiful.
I like what you like.
I am your best friend.
You cannot shake me off.
I never die.
You are the outside of me.
I am always with you.
I am what you are.
What am I?

Answer: Your soul.

Anukriti Barot (6)
Gearies Primary School, Gants Hill

The Crossing

It's black like ink and it's white like a polar bear.
It's stripy like a rainbow.
It begins with a "Z"
It's a crossing.
They eat grass too.
They can live in the zoo with lots of animals.
They might have people to look after the huge animal.
What am I?

Answer: A zebra.

Aarshika Kokulan (6)
Gearies Primary School, Gants Hill

The King

I am bright, soft, furry and yellow.
I have a massive mane as spiky as a toothbrush.
I am as massive as a gigantic dinosaur.
I am as ferocious as a tiger.
I have a roar as loud as a house breaking.
I have very spiky teeth.
What am I?

Answer: A lion.

Sukhvir Singh Bassi (7)
Gearies Primary School, Gants Hill

The Mysterious Animal

I am white as snow.
I eat strange food,
I am cute, soft and nice.
I jump high as a tiger jumping high in the air.
I like to eat carrots.
I am a fast runner.
I have light pink on my toes.
I have big round eyes.
What am I?

Answer: A rabbit.

Liyana Khan (6)
Gearies Primary School, Gants Hill

The Strange Thing

I have sharp, pointy and shiny teeth.
I have a beautiful yellow crown.
I love to eat meat, so I am a carnivore.
I am very fierce like a dragon.
When I was born, I was called a cub.
The lady does not have much fur.
What am I?

Answer: A lion.

Krithi Rao Erabelli (7)
Gearies Primary School, Gants Hill

The Wiggle Thing

I am pink and wiggle.
You can see me on beaches.
But sometimes you can see me in the ocean.
I've got four daddy long legs.
I have a shell like a turtle.
When you step on me I will hurt you.
What am I?

Answer: A jellyfish.

Milly Nakum (7)
Gearies Primary School, Gants Hill

Orange And Spotty Animal

I am very spotty like a hyena.
I am very fast like a lion.
I begin with a C.
I eat a gazelle for my prey.
I can be eaten by a lion if it can catch me.
My claws are sharp as razor-sharp teeth.
What am I?

Answer: A cheetah.

Atharv Jadhav (7)
Gearies Primary School, Gants Hill

What Am I?

I am as colourful as a rainbow shining.
I eat fish and mice.
My coat is fluffy and soft.
My whiskers are not short.
My bed is nice, soft and cushiony.
My teeth are sharp.
My eyes are small.
What am I?

Answer: A cat.

Inayah Iffat Hussain (7)
Gearies Primary School, Gants Hill

The Reflection Keeper

When you go in front of me, you will see yourself.
You can put me anywhere, not outside.
I'm like a picture but without the photo.
I have four sides.
I have metal or wood around me.
What am I?

Answer: A mirror.

Rayyan Mukhtar (7)
Gearies Primary School, Gants Hill

The Creepy Thing

I am as ferocious as a wolf.
I love to hunt for predators.
I love meat.
I am yellow as a giraffe.
I am powerful and have four legs.
I have sharp claws that are as sharp as a knife.
What am I?

Answer: A lion.

Nadia Suleyman (7)
Gearies Primary School, Gants Hill

The Sweet

I am very sticky and round.
I am as sticky as a sticky road being built.
I am brown, yellow, green and pink.
I am round and I have a stick at the bottom.
I come in different sizes.
What am I?

Answer: A lollipop.

Josh Wigham (6)
Gearies Primary School, Gants Hill

The Mischievous King

I eat meat.
I am as green and blue as the fishes.
I am as rough as the scales of the fishes.
My teeth are twice as sharp as the crocodiles.
I am as mischievous as the thieves.
What am I?

Answer: The Dragon King.

Aarav Ravikiran (7)
Gearies Primary School, Gants Hill

A Long Horn

I am a myth.
I'm like a horse with a horn.
I make more magic than a wand.
I gallop faster than a race car.
I start with a "U".
I am white with pink sparkles.
What am I?

Answer: A unicorn.

Anshika Sinha (6)
Gearies Primary School, Gants Hill

The High Jumper

I jump very high.
I never get tired.
I am sweet and smooth.
I come in different types of brown colours.
I have big long legs.
On my head I have something that's tall.
What am I?

Answer: A bunny.

Sukaina Shanawaz (7)
Gearies Primary School, Gants Hill

The Cheating Choice

I am as soft as a bunny.
I am as fluffy as fur.
I am as yellow as the sun.
I am as fast as a lion.
I am as spotty as spots.
I have paws as sharp as a knife
What am I?

Answer: A cheetah.

Aileen Ahmed (7)
Gearies Primary School, Gants Hill

The Round Pink Thing

It is round and you lick it.
It is sweet and slippery on top.
It is small and as soft as a teddy bear.
It can be any colour and it begins with an "L".
What is it?

Answer: A lollipop.

Avneet Kaur Bansal (6)
Gearies Primary School, Gants Hill

The Bouncy Thing

I hop around everywhere.
I am grey and white.
I have a pink nose.
I have whiskers next to my nose.
Most of the time I smile a lot.
I have sharp claws.
What am I?

Answer: A bunny.

Eshaal Shah (6)
Gearies Primary School, Gants Hill

The Scary Thing

I am scary and strong.
I have spiky claws.
I am furry and ferocious.
I'm always hungry.
I am huge.
I live in a forest.
I am smelly too.
What am I?

Answer: A bear.

Zakariya Mughal (7)
Gearies Primary School, Gants Hill

The Flying Thing

My wings are bigger than a bird.
I come in the dark.
I have beautiful colours.
I breathe hot red fire colours.
I sit on the eggs until they hatch.
What am I?

Answer: A dragon.

Aniya Rahman (7)
Gearies Primary School, Gants Hill

The Hairy Creature

I am very hairy and scary.
I feed on small insects.
I have a very nasty sting.
I am as small as an ant.
I live everywhere specially on trees.
What am I?

Answer: A tarantula.

Faisal Shaikh (7)
Gearies Primary School, Gants Hill

Messy Things

I am not the best at doing stuff.
I love eating.
I'm smelly too.
People make me upset.
People spend lots of time with me.
People love me
What am I?

Answer: A baby.

Oluwaseyi Rebecca Olukoshi (6)
Gearies Primary School, Gants Hill

The Orange Thing

I have eight legs.
I swim in the water.
I have a huge head and huge eyes.
I am orange.
I am like sticky jelly.
I am as fast as a car.
What am I?

Answer: An octopus.

Reyansh Singh (6)
Gearies Primary School, Gants Hill

The Mighty Thing

I am an evil mighty beast.
I am lots of shiny red colours.
I am ferocious.
I eat meat.
I breathe hot red fire.
I have huge wings.
What am I?

Answer: A dragon.

Rayyanah Rahman (6)
Gearies Primary School, Gants Hill

The Wing

I begin with an "E"
I have black and white feathers.
I have two dark yellow feet.
I fly in the sky.
I lay my eggs in my nest
What am I?

Answer: An eagle.

Nathan Joshua Sarusan Suthushan (7)
Gearies Primary School, Gants Hill

The Krill Eater

I'm blue as the big blue sea.
I'm a gentle giant.
My body fat is called blubber.
I don't have teeth.
I won't eat you.
What am I?

Answer: A whale.

Moses Kwok (7)
Gearies Primary School, Gants Hill

The Ringing Thing

I ring loud like a bell.
I play really fun games.
I live in an old pocket or a new pocket.
I talk to chatty people and listen to people.
What am I?

Answer: iPhone X

Haniah Khan (7)
Gearies Primary School, Gants Hill

What Am I?

I like bananas.
I am brown and soft.
I play in the zoo.
I feel soft as a blanket.
I am brown as a bear.
I live in the zoo.
What am I?

Answer: A monkey.

Jannat Ali (7)
Gearies Primary School, Gants Hill

Swim Away

I can swim underwater,
I can paddle,
I have an orange beak.
I am fluffy.
I look like a swan.
I eat fish from the lake.
What am I?

Answer: A penguin.

Nikita Rayanagoudar (6)
Gearies Primary School, Gants Hill

Animal Or Rock?

I am a light orange colour.
I have black and orange fur.
I have very sharp claws like needles.
I have sharp teeth like a knife.
What am I?

Answer: A tiger.

Sneha Chawla (7)
Gearies Primary School, Gants Hill

Nine Lives

I love to play with little bitty balls.
I use claws to scratch wooden doors.
I eat fish.
I lick myself.
I live in houses.
What am I?

Answer: A cat.

Zakariya Ajaib (6)
Gearies Primary School, Gants Hill

King Of The Jungle

I am shiny like a cheetah.
I am as strong as a tiger.
I am nearly as loud as a bear.
My eyes are yellow, shiny like a sun.
What am I?

Answer: A lion.

Jake Sivadasan (6)
Gearies Primary School, Gants Hill

King Of The Jungle

I live in the jungle.
I eat meat.
I have soft orangy brown fur.
I run fast.
I can jump very high.
I am strong.
What am I?

Answer: A tiger.

Rahim Khan (6)
Gearies Primary School, Gants Hill

The Hot Bird

My wings are big.
I am hot like a volcano.
From the ashes, I'm reborn.
I have two legs.
I am very beautiful.
What am I?

Answer: A phoenix.

Yan Mellies (6)
Gearies Primary School, Gants Hill

The Enormous Fish

I live in the deep blue sea.
I am very dangerous.
I have sharp teeth.
I am grey and my skin is smooth.
I eat fish.
What am I?

Answer: A shark.

Eesa Koreshi (6)
Gearies Primary School, Gants Hill

What Am I?

I have four wheels.
I come in lots of different incredible colours.
I go really fast like a flash.
I am really powerful.
What am I?

Answer: A car.

Hamza Musa Islam (6)
Gearies Primary School, Gants Hill

The Long Thing

I am very long, gigantic and massive.
I live in a weird school.
I am as tall as a giant.
I have lots of spots.
What am I?

Answer: A bead string.

Usaud Abdul-Hafiz (7)
Gearies Primary School, Gants Hill

The Important Person

I am important like the Queen.
I judge England.
I work for the Queen.
I am the Prime Minister.
I am fancy.
Who am I?

Answer: Mrs May.

Judi Ibrahim (6)
Gearies Primary School, Gants Hill

Mrs Fluffy

I have long ears
I'm white and fluffy.
I can move my nose.
I love yummy carrots.
I jump and hop
What am I?

Answer: A bunny.

Huma Ali (7)
Gearies Primary School, Gants Hill

McDonald's Sauce

I am delicious to eat.
I am red and opaque.
I am a sauce.
I begin with a "S"
What am I?

Answer: Sweet chilli sauce.

Ethan Arifin (7)
Gearies Primary School, Gants Hill

Fast And Clever

I have a soft furry coat.
I enjoy a healthy diet.
I have long spiky whiskers.
I have to keep my claws short.
I have a cute twitching nose.
I bounce and stretch every day.
What am I?

Answer: A rabbit.

Vinnie Essex (6)
Holy Family Catholic Primary School, Benfleet

Cover

I give comfort.
People come to me during rain and snow.
I can stand in the middle of the forest and the city.
I look beautiful during Christmas.
I can be warm inside.
What am I?

Answer: A house.

John Desireoluwa Akinlabi (6)
Holy Family Catholic Primary School, Benfleet

Unlock

I am a hard shiny object.
I can be silver or gold.
I am all different shapes, but can fit in a hole.
I can be used to keep a secret.
And to keep a room closed.
What am I?

Answer: A key.

Elsie Mae Marsh (5)
Holy Family Catholic Primary School, Benfleet

Sneaky

I have yellow fur with black spots.
I have eyes that look like I am crying.
I like to eat meat.
I am the fastest land animal in the world.
I live in Africa.
What am I?

Answer: A cheetah.

Sam Chittock (5)
Holy Family Catholic Primary School, Benfleet

Poison

I live in Australia.
I am poisonous.
There are lots of us.
I am black.
I have legs each side of my body.
You can actually find us in any country.
What am I?

Answer: A spider.

Milly McMeekin (6)
Holy Family Catholic Primary School, Benfleet

Web Power

I am small.
I come in different colours.
I live in your house.
I sometimes put a spin on things.
I like to eat insects.
I have eight legs.
What am I?

Answer: A spider.

Jamie Scott (6)
Holy Family Catholic Primary School, Benfleet

Jumpy

I am always friendly.
I can lick my eyes.
I move slow and fast.
My skin is scaly.
I am so still.
I jump high
What am I?

Answer: A crested gecko.

Pearse Mastrogiacomo (6)
Holy Family Catholic Primary School, Benfleet

Glide

I am scary,
I have sharp claws.
My body is long.
I move very fast.
I am very fierce.
I am really evil.
What am I?

Answer: An eagle.

Alfie Robert Thomas (5)
Holy Family Catholic Primary School, Benfleet

Claw

I am hairy.
I have sharp claws.
I'm long.
I have a yellow face.
I am fast.
I have an orange tail.
What am I?

Answer: A lion.

Sam Starling (6)
Holy Family Catholic Primary School, Benfleet

Swing

I am green.
My body is scaly.
I have a long tail
I move fast.
I am sticky.
My body is smooth
What am I?

Answer: A chameleon.

Winnie Campbell (5)
Holy Family Catholic Primary School, Benfleet

Jolly

I am red.
I am old.
I live in the North Pole.
I am friendly.
I have a bag.
I have lots of helpers.
Who am I?

Answer: Santa.

Antonio Patron Fajardo (6)
Holy Family Catholic Primary School, Benfleet

Fast

I am fluffy and soft.
I'm brown and some are white.
I am beautiful.
I am hairy.
I am nice.
What am I?

Answer: A horse.

Alicja Macleod (6)
Holy Family Catholic Primary School, Benfleet

Cold

I am long.
I am very hard.
I can be white.
I keep people warm.
Sometimes I'm cold.
What am I?

Answer: A radiator.

Isabella Welling (6)
Holy Family Catholic Primary School, Benfleet

Hairy

I am fast.
I am yellow.
My face is scary.
I am hairy.
I have sharp teeth.
I am long.
What am I?

Answer: A lion.

Leo Hanby (6)
Holy Family Catholic Primary School, Benfleet

Fly

I am colourful.
I am flappy.
I am slow.
I am smooth.
I am soft.
I am dotty.
What am I?

Answer: A butterfly.

Olivia Hope Ladyko (6)
Holy Family Catholic Primary School, Benfleet

Old

I am old
I am friendly.
My clothes are red.
I am jolly.
I am tall.
I am peachy.
Who am I?

Answer: Santa.

Simon Patron Fajardo (6)
Holy Family Catholic Primary School, Benfleet

Little Riddlers 2018 - Essex

Jumpy

I am long.
I am jumpy.
I am scaly.
I am green.
I am wet.
I'm smooth.
What am I?

Answer: A frog.

Tia Lily O'Callaghan (5)
Holy Family Catholic Primary School, Benfleet

Shiny

I am hard.
I am sharp
I am cold.
I am shiny.
I am sparkly.
I am round.
What am I?

Answer: A ring.

Casper James Saban (5)
Holy Family Catholic Primary School, Benfleet

Soft

I am long.
I am fast.
My body is brown.
I am friendly.
I am fluffy.
What am I?

Answer: A reindeer.

Ishika Jibi (6)
Holy Family Catholic Primary School, Benfleet

Small

I am small
I am black.
My babies are tiny.
I am a nice creature.
What am I?

Answer: An ant.

Roman Overall (5)
Holy Family Catholic Primary School, Benfleet

Long

I run fast.
I have long legs
I have spots.
I live in Africa.
What am I?

Answer: A giraffe.

Tilly Witherall-Gosling (5)
Holy Family Catholic Primary School, Benfleet

Marvellous Marsupial

I'm a marsupial and I'm a little medium mammal.
I move by using sharp claws and rough pads.
I am called a Joey as a little baby.
I did not come from an egg.
I live in Australia and nearby Islands.
I am a land animal.
I'm a species of bear.
You can tell the difference between male and female.
I have fluffy ears and yellow eyes.
What am I?

Answer: A koala.

Reece Oliver Newcombe (7)
Ingrave Johnstone CE Primary, Brentwood

Hairy Business

I am a big mammal.
I can grow up to 1.8 metres
I have small ears, but I can hear well.
I live in the wild only in Africa.
I often walk on all fours,
But, I can walk upright.
My powerful arms are longer than my legs.
I munch tough stems, juicy shoots, leaves and fruit.
Babies start to crawl about nine weeks old.
What am I?

Answer: A gorilla.

Andrew Scott Gordon (7)
Ingrave Johnstone CE Primary, Brentwood

Jump

I am amphibian,
So, I can live on land and in water.
I was born in a egg.
The size of me is eight to eleven cm long.
I have really big eyes and a flat head.
I can live almost all around the world.
I am happy splashing in the water.
I can jump twenty times my body length.
I eat flies.
What am I?

Answer: A frog.

Lily Millington (6)
Ingrave Johnstone CE Primary, Brentwood

Flying High

I come out of an egg.
I eat different food at different times.
My body length is up to three cm.
My wingspan is up to ten cm.
I am very colourful.
I am an insect.
I move by flapping my wings up and down.
I'm found in most parts of the world.
I have long and beautiful wings.
What am I?

Answer: A butterfly.

Matilda Rose Woodhouse (6)
Ingrave Johnstone CE Primary, Brentwood

Claws

I am a marsupial.
I have strong arms and legs.
Clawed feet to climb trees.
I grow up to 60cm long.
I live in the wild in Australia and nearby lands.
I live in my mummy's pouch as a baby.
I have sharp claws and rough pads on my paws.
I look like a small cuddly bear.
What am I?

Answer: A koala.

Harley Emmie Brandon (6)
Ingrave Johnstone CE Primary, Brentwood

Fierce Mammal

I move with my strong legs.
I can grow up to six feet tall.
I eat plants and meat.
I live in North America, Russia and Japan.
I came out of my mum's tummy.
I am a mammal.
I have four legs and I can stand on two.
I am big, brown and hairy.
I am an animal.
What am I?

Answer: A brown bear.

Adam Staunton (7)
Ingrave Johnstone CE Primary, Brentwood

Frosty Fingers!

I am a mammal.
I have sharp teeth.
I can walk on ice and water.
I can eat seals.
In the summer I eat lemmings, birds and fish.
I live in the Arctic.
I have babies.
I am not cuddly.
The size is 25-3m and 2-2.5m big claws.
What am I?

Answer: A polar bear.

Ronnie Tyler Smale (7)
Ingrave Johnstone CE Primary, Brentwood

Scales

I'm over seven metres long.
I eat insects, fish and crabs.
I live in Asia, America and Australia.
I am a reptile.
I swim using my powerful tail.
I have my tail to keep my body up.
I can run and walk on land.
What am I?

Answer: A crocodile.

Dylan Balroop (7)
Ingrave Johnstone CE Primary, Brentwood

What Am I?

I come from a small egg
I eat anything
I am an omnivore.
I am long like a hand.
I live in Africa.
I have scaly skin.
I move by grasping branches with my clawed feet and gripping tail.
I can change colours.
What am I?

Answer: A chameleon.

Dylan Fox (7)
Ingrave Johnstone CE Primary, Brentwood

Yum, Yum

I'm a mammal.
I live in Asia and Africa.
I can run up to 65km over short distances.
I am a meat eater.
I can grow up to 1.3 metres,
My tail length up to 1.4 metres.
I am a member of the Panthera family
What am I?

Answer: A tiger.

Nikita Jarkov (7)
Ingrave Johnstone CE Primary, Brentwood

Growl

I move by using my sharp claws.
My spotty coat keeps me hidden in the grass.
I am six metres with a long tail.
I live in Asia and Africa.
My mum gave birth to live young.
I am not a fussy eater.
What am I?

Answer: A leopard.

Finley Pamment (6)
Ingrave Johnstone CE Primary, Brentwood

Furry Animals

I'm a mammal.
I have a black and white coat.
I live in China and my country is warm.
I can climb high trees.
I walk on strong branches.
I am cute and fluffy.
Mum gave birth to me.
What am I?

Answer: A panda.

Frankie Towner (6)
Ingrave Johnstone CE Primary, Brentwood

Roam The Trees Of Australia

I live in Australia.
I am a marsupial
I don't have very good eyesight.
But can hear very well.
I came out of my mum's belly.
I am a fussy eater.
I eat eucalyptus trees.
What am I?

Answer: A koala.

Daniel Retief (7)
Ingrave Johnstone CE Primary, Brentwood

Wiggle

I didn't enter the world as an egg.
I am a small mammal.
I don't live in Africa.
I eat seeds, nuts and fruit.
I can be red or brown.
I scamper from branch to branch.
What am I?

Answer: A squirrel.

Elizabeth Ellery (7)
Ingrave Johnstone CE Primary, Brentwood

Click, Clack

I live in many countries of North America
and Asia.
I eat meat.
I have big teeth.
I have fur, so I am a mammal.
I have a great sense of smell.
I didn't hatch from a egg.
What am I?

Answer: A wolf.

Frankie Harris (7)
Ingrave Johnstone CE Primary, Brentwood

Little Riddlers 2018 - Essex

Stripes

I live in Africa.
I eat grass.
I have black and white stripes.
My mummy gave birth to me.
We run in a herd.
I am a mammal.
What am I?

Answer: A zebra.

Sehej Jutley (7)
Ingrave Johnstone CE Primary, Brentwood

YoungWriters
Est.1991

YOUNG WRITERS INFORMATION

We hope you have enjoyed reading this book – and that you will continue to in the coming years.

If you're a young writer who enjoys reading and creative writing, or the parent of an enthusiastic poet or story writer, do visit our website **www.youngwriters.co.uk**. Here you will find free competitions, workshops and games, as well as recommended reads, a poetry glossary and our blog.

If you would like to order further copies of this book, or any of our other titles, then please give us a call or visit **www.youngwriters.co.uk**.

Young Writers
Remus House
Coltsfoot Drive
Peterborough
PE2 9BF
(01733) 890066
info@youngwriters.co.uk